D0745372

CONTENTS

"Forever Plaid" opened May 20, 1990 at Steve McGraw's, New York City

Logo Design: Mark Horton
Cover Photo © 1991 Martha Swope Associates/Photo credit: Carol Rosegg

THE DEDICATION

 is dedicated to the good guys:

—To the guys who wheeled the projector carts for the Audio Visual Club

—To the guys who carried an extra white handkerchief in the back pockets of their chinos

—To the guys who saved their allowances to give their parents an extra special night on the town for their anniversary

—To the guys who sang around the piano in the family room just for the love of it

—To the guys who never went beyond first base (and if by some miracle they did, they didn't tell anyone). We salute you!

When most of us think of the 1950's, we think of Rock 'n' Roll, greasers, hot rods, Elvis, Annette, Fabian, D.A. haircuts and teenage rebellion. But there was a "flipside" to this era — the side of harmony, innocence and the sincerity of dreams. It is the side that's been lost in the shuffle of progress. It was a time when most parents and kids listened and danced tot he same music; when families partook of the ritual of gathering in front of the TV to watch their favorite variety shows, like the Ed Sullivan Show or the Perry Como Show. It was a time when every family worked hard to fulfill the American dream.

It was a period when Four-Part Guy Groups harmonized their way across the airwaves, jukeboxes, and hi-fi's of the country. Throughout the land they would stand at a quartet of microphones, crooning a multitude of chaperoned prom-goers into dreamy romance.

They wore dinner jackets and bow ties (or, perhaps, cardigans and white bucks). Each move was drilled to precision. Each vocal arrangement soared to stratospheric heights of harmony. This sound crested right before Rock 'n' Roll stole the heartbeat of music across the globe.

During this time, guys across the country banded together to sing in the basement for fun. If things worked out they might be hired to sing at weddings, conventions, proms and country club socials. Inspired by the success of the recording stars, they made plans to zoom into careers of fame and fortune. But the musical taste of the USA was changing, and would not stop to listen to their dreams. This is the story of such a group — **FOREVER PLAID**.

Once upon a time, there were four guys (Sparky, Smudge, Jinx and Frankie) who loved to sing. They all met in high school, when they joined the Audio Visual Club (1956). Discovering that they shared an affection for music and entertaining, they got together and dreamed of becoming like their idols — The Four Aces, The Four Lads, The Four Freshmen, The Hi-Lo's and The Crew Cuts. They rehearsed in the basement of Smudge's family's plumbing supply company. It was here they became **FOREVER PLAID** — a name that connotes the continuation of traditional values, of family, home and harmony. Although Rock 'n' Roll was racing down the fast lane like a candy-apple "VETTE", they believed in their music. As their sound developed, they sang at family gatherings, fund raisers and eventually graduated to supermarket openings and proms. They had little time for romance or leisure for they supported their fantasy by holding down "day" jobs — Frankie was in dental supplies, Jinx was into auto parts, Smudge was in bathroom fixtures, Sparky was in better dresses. They devoted themselves to their singing at nights and on weekends. Then, finally, they landed their first big gig at the Airport Hilton Cocktail Bar — THE FUSEL-LOUNGE (February 9, 1964).

En route to pick up their custom-made Plaid Tuxedoes, they were slammed broadside by a school bus filled with eager Catholic teens. The teens were on their way to witness the Beatles make their US television debut on the Ed Sullivan Show and, miraculously, escaped uninjured. The members of **FOREVER PLAID** were killed instantly. It is at the moment when their careers and lives ended, that the story of **FOREVER PLAID** begins.

Through the Power of Harmony and the Expanding Holes in the Ozone Layer in conjunction with the position of the Planets and all that Astro-Technical stuff, they are allowed to come back to perform the show they never got to do in life (and record the album they always dreamed of making).

And, having completed their mission of Harmony, our men in plaid must return to the cosmos. Although they may be gone, through this show their dreams live on forever...

A *FEW WORDS FROM OUR MEN IN PLAID.*
Dear Listener,
We've been asked to write a few words about our show. Since we're only on this planet for a short while, we'll be brief. O.K.?

THREE COINS IN THE FOUNTAIN — *We chose this 1954 Academy Award winner as our opening number for its sincere longing for happiness and romance. Frankie takes the lead. (He won the toss.)*
* GOTTA BE THIS OR THAT / UNDECIDED — *Two classic jump tunes that segue into each other. Segue is music 'lingo' for singing two songs without any yakkin' between them.*

MOMENTS REMEMBER — *This song unleashes all the cascading memories and feelings of that most crucial event in all our lives...the Prom.*
CRAZY 'BOUT YA, BABY — *The sentiments of this song, while peppy, are true. We love doin' this one. We just love it. We used to rehearse this in the basement of Smudge's Plumbing Supply Company practicing with bathroom plungers as microphones till we could afford real mikes. So, if you listen carefully, you may hear 'em.*

NO, NOT MUCH! — *Although we never had any true romance in life, (we were always so busy working and rehearsing — and Sparky with his speech therapy after school), we would reveal our feelings of true love through our music.*

* PERFIDIA — *We dedicate this to our Spanish teacher, Senorita PaFuentes, who was the third runner up in the Miss Rheingold Contest. (She was one of the first advocates of the Audio Lingual Method of learning a foreign tongue. So we all invested in these language records. Let's see if that investment paid off.)*

CRY — *The quintessential statement of lost 'amore', lost hope and new beginnings. This is Jinx's big feature. We hope he doesn't get a nosebleed when he goes for the big ending.*

SIXTEEN TONS / *CHAIN GANG— *Though we work hard singing about men who love, we love singing about men who work — hard.*

* A TRIBUTE TO MR. C — *One sultry night Perry Como was stranded in our town and caught our show at the bowling alley. When it was over he gave us his golden cardigan. Perry, this song has your name on it.*

* OUR CARIBBEAN MEDLEY — *We wish you could see the neat props we use during this our Calypso fiesta. We have these bananas and jalapeno peppers that light up, and we wear these big hats with fringe. It's great. For the full effect, please join in on the chorus. (Thanks Harry). Here are the words: "MATILDA, MATILDA, MATILDA SHE TAKE ME MONEY AND RUN VENEZUELA" (Pretty simple, huh)*

HEART AND SOUL — *Sparky tickles the ivories while Frankie croons the lead. Everyone knows either the top or the bottom part on the piano so play along with us. Unless you're listening to this in your car or something.*

* LADY OF SPAIN — *Jinx sings his lungs out and plays his trusty accordion, while the rest of us present the entire Ed Sullivan Show behind his back. Don't tell him.*

* SCOTLAND THE BRAVE — *Although none of us is Scottish, we do pay homage to our name which means — according to the dictionary — 'PLAID (plad)n A woven cloth, traditionally worn over the left shoulder. This Highlander material is comprised of a series of cross-barred patterns and colorful squares, signifying family and home.' We would like to add — "friendship."*

SHANGRI-LA/RAGS TO RICHES — *Shangri-La is that special place where mankind may find eternal peace & happiness. And from whence come our long-awaited plaid tuxedoes. They are truly the most beautiful jackets in men's fashion history.*

LOVE IS A MANY SPLENDORED THING — *Our Anthem and our Finale. We really don't want to sing this because, when we finish the last chord, we'll have to go back — perhaps forever. So, we'll sign off for now and say thank you for reading all this.*

Plaidly,

Frankie
Sparky
Jinx
Smudge

* Not included in this collection.

THREE COINS IN THE FOUNTAIN

Words by
SAMMY CAHN

Music by
JULE STYNE

Which one will the foun-tain bless? Which one will the foun-tain

bless? THREE COINS IN THE FOUN-TAIN, Through the rip-ples how they

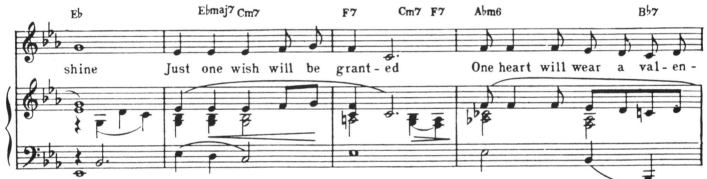

shine Just one wish will be grant-ed One heart will wear a val-en-

tine. Make it mine! Make it mine! Make it

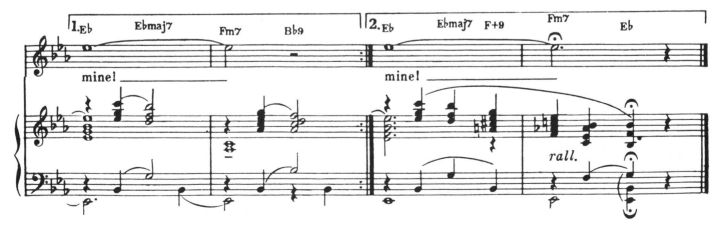

mine! mine!

MOMENTS TO REMEMBER

Words by
AL STILLMAN

Music by
ROBERT ALLEN

MO-MENTS TO RE-MEM - BER. Tho' sum-mer turns to win-ter and the

pre - sent dis - ap - pears, The laugh-ter we were glad to share will

e - cho thru the years. When oth - er nights and oth - er days may

find us gone our sep'-rate ways, We will have these MO-MENTS TO RE -

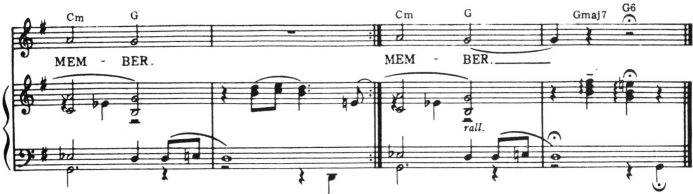

1.
MEM - BER.

2.
MEM - BER.

CRAZY 'BOUT YA, BABY

Words by
PAT BARRETT

Music by
RUDI MAUGERI

Moderate Boogie Woogie

Cra - zy 'bout ya, ba - by, want ya all to my - self,
time has come, my hon - ey, will you please be my wife,
Af - ter we are mar - ried, we will raise a fam - i - ly,

cra - zy 'bout ya, ba - by, no - one else on the shelf.
I will take good care of you the rest of your life.
all the plans we had be - fore will fit right to a tee.

Give me all your lov - ing, all that you can af - ford, _____
Gon - na spend a lot - ta mon - ey, house built for two, _____ a
We'll be liv - in' hum - ble in our own lit - tle way, _____ if

let me keep you al - ways ev - er to be a - dored.
cot - tage in the coun - try___ for just me and you.
we're to be so for - tu - nate, pray this be the day.

Refrain

Cra - zy 'bout ya, ba - by, ___ cra - zy 'bout ya, ba - by, ___

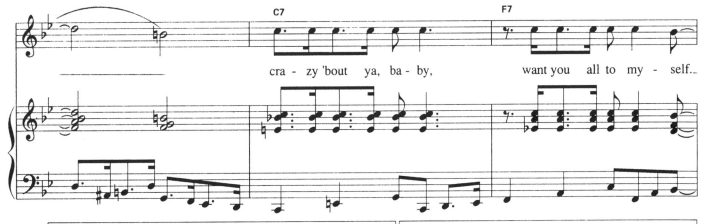

___ cra - zy 'bout ya, ba - by, want you all to my - self.___

The

NO, NOT MUCH!

Words by
AL STILLMAN

Music by
ROBERT ALLEN

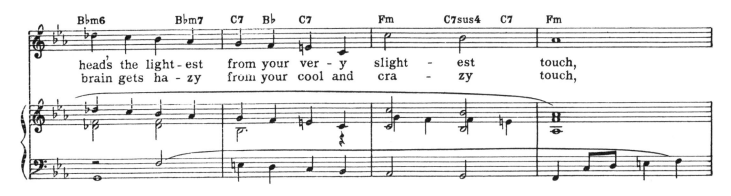

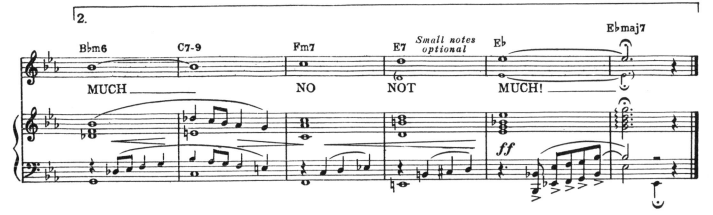

CRY

Words and Music by
CHURCHILL KOHLMAN

feel! _____ If your heart-aches seem to hang a - round too long, _____

_____ And your blues keep get-ting blu - er with each song _____ Re-

mem-ber, sun-shine can be found be - hind a cloud-y sky, So let your hair down and go

on and CRY. _____ If your CRY. _____

SIXTEEN TONS

Words and Music by
MERLE TRAVIS

mind _____ that's _____ weak _____ and a back that's strong. You load
straw - boss _____ said _____ "Well - a bless my soul." You load
high - toned _____ wo - man make me walk the line. You load
right one don't - a get you, then the left one will. You load

Chorus

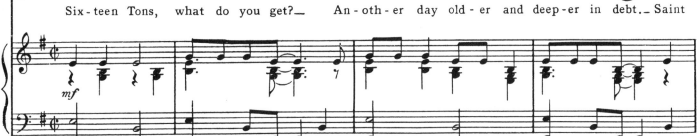

Six-teen Tons, what do you get?_ An - oth - er day old - er and deep-er in debt._ Saint

Pe -ter, don't you call me 'cause I can't go_ I owe_ my soul to the com - pa - ny store._

1. 2. 3. | **4.**

2. I was
3. I was
4. If you

CATCH A FALLING STAR

Words and Music by
PAUL VANCE and LEE POCKRISS

HEART AND SOUL

Words by
FRANK LOESSER

Music by
HOAGY CARMICHAEL

Refrain
Moderato, Not Too Fast, Lightly Rhythmical

UNDECIDED

Words by
SID ROBIN

Music by
CHARLES SHAVERS

Refrain

First you say you do and then you don't,— and then you say you will and

then you won't.— You're UN-DE-CI-DED now, so what are you gon-na do?—

Now you want to play, and then it's no,— and when you say you'll stay, that's

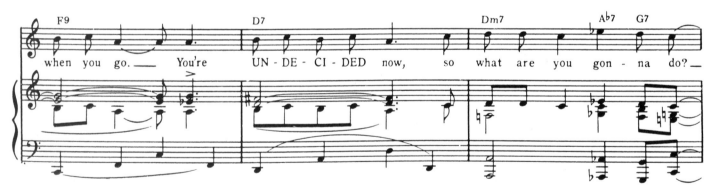

when you go.— You're UN-DE-CI-DED now, so what are you gon-na do?—

I've been sit-ting on a fence, and it does-n't make much sense,'cause you

keep me in sus-pense and you know it.___ Then you prom-ise to re-turn. When you

don't, I real-ly burn. Well, I guess I'll nev-er learn, and I show it. ___

If you've got a heart and if you're kind, _ then don't keep us a-part. Make

up your mind. You're UN - DE - CI - DED now, so what are you gon-na do?_

SHANGRI-LA

Lyrics by
CARL SIGMAN

Music by
MATT MALNECK and ROBERT MAXWELL

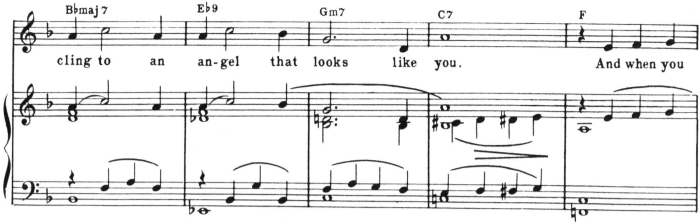

cling to an an-gel that looks like you. And when you

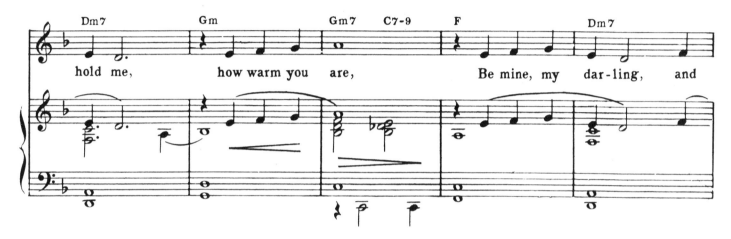

hold me, how warm you are, Be mine, my dar-ling, and

spend your life with me in SHAN-GRI - LA,_____ For an-y-where you

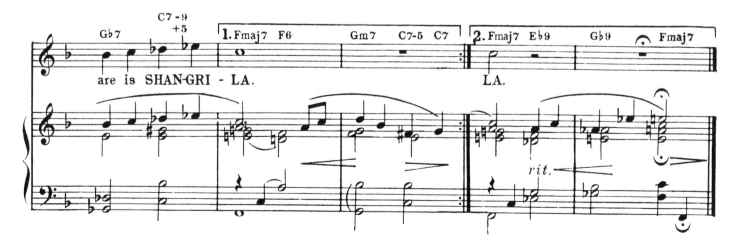

are is SHAN-GRI - LA. LA.

RAGS TO RICHES

Words and Music by
RICHARD ADLER and JERRY ROSS

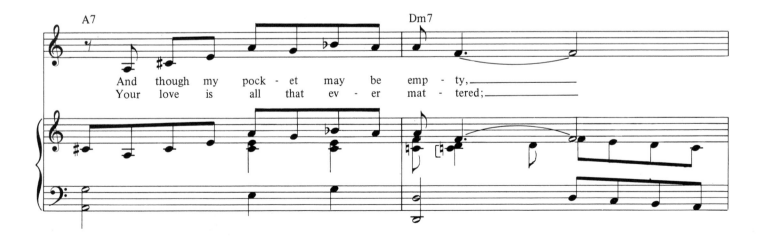

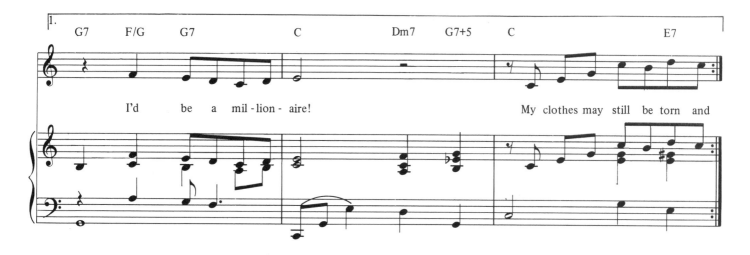

1. I'd be a mil-lion-aire! My clothes may still be torn and

2. it's ev-'ry-thing. So

With a bolero feel

o-pen your arms and you'll o-pen the door to all the trea-sures that

I'm hop-ing for. Hold me and kiss me and tell me you're mine ev-er-

28

more! Must I for-ev-er stay a beg-gar

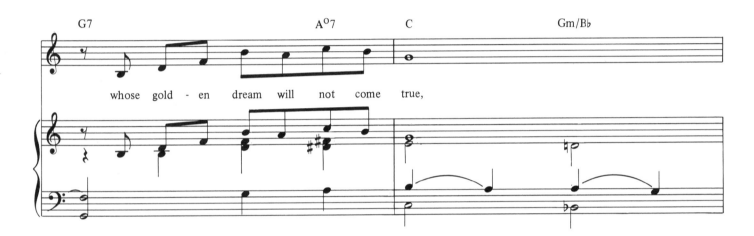

whose gold - en dream will not come true,

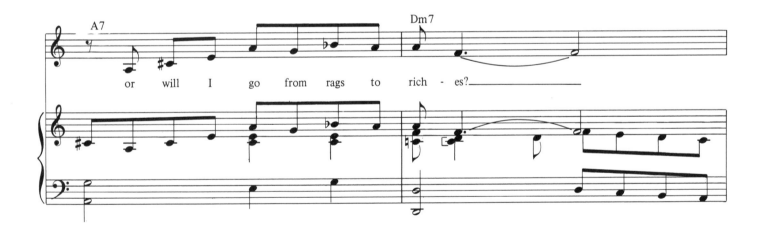

or will I go from rags to rich - es?

My fate is up to you!

LOVE IS A MANY SPLENDORED THING

Lyrics by
PAUL FRANCIS WEBSTER

Music by
SAMMY FAIN

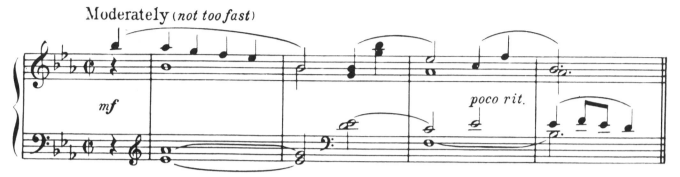

town, _____ And I said, "Can you tell me, please, ___

___ where's that love I've nev-er found? _____ Un - rav - el me this

rid - dle. what is love? What can it be?" And

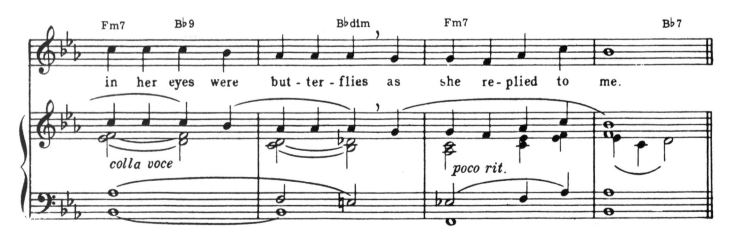

in her eyes were but - ter - flies as she re - plied to me.

Refrain, Moderately (*not too fast*)

LOVE _____ IS A MAN-Y-SPLEN-DORED THING, ___ It's the

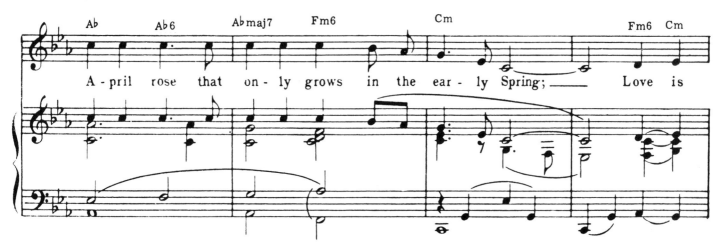

A - pril rose that on-ly grows in the ear-ly Spring; ___ Love is

na - ture's way of giv-ing a rea-son to be liv-ing, The

gold - en crown that makes a man a king. _____